# The God Story
## Daily Readings

## Jacob Armstrong

*Abingdon Press*
Nashville

THE GOD STORY: DAILY READINGS
by Jacob Armstrong

Copyright © 2013 by Abingdon Press
All rights reserved.

*This book is printed on acid-free, elemental chlorine-free paper.*

Library of Congress Cataloging-in-Publication applied for.

ISBN 978-1-4267-7379-2

13 14 15 16 17 18 19 20 21 22—10 9 8 7 6 5 4 3 2 1

MANUFACTURED IN THE UNITED STATES OF AMERICA

# Contents

# Welcome to
# the God Story

I remember a conversation I had with my dad when I was eight or nine years old. We were sitting on our front porch in old wood rocking chairs. It's an interesting memory for me because I have very few of the front porch; it wasn't a common place for us to spend our time. But on this day it was just Dad and me on the front porch. I had been trying to find the courage to tell my dad something that I thought he would tell me was foolish or childish. On the front porch that day, I mustered up the courage to tell him something that I thought made me weird, something I would never have told my friends. I figured he could tell me how to stop, how to grow up.

"Dad, I feel like my life is a movie or a great story. I pretend. A lot. I pretend that I am the hero of my story and there are bad guys and good guys, and I fight for the good side, of course. Even at school or Cub Scouts or wherever, I'm pretending it is part of my adventure, my story, of which I am the star."

I didn't tell him anything about my thoughts of damsels in distress, or my deep fear of the enemy. I didn't tell him everything. I told him a little and waited for him to reason with me. I waited for him to share logic with me to help me get out of my fairy tale.

Staring out into the field across from our house, never looking at me, my dad replied, "Yeah, me too."

G.K. Chesterton said, "I had always felt life first as a story: and if there is a story there is a story-teller."[1]

My dad's affirmation that day would grow into my belief today that I am indeed a part of a greater story, a story with good guys and bad guys, adventure and romance, intrigue and suspense.

I am a part of the God Story and you are too.

It can be easy to look at the Bible as a haphazard collection of sixty-six books from different eras, different regimes, and different authors, written with different intents.

It can equally be easy to see our fragmented lives as a haphazard collection of events with little to nothing holding it all together.

Neither one of these vantage points is accurate.

I believe your life changes when you see the threads that run through the great story of God's people found in the Bible, and when you see your life as a continuation of that story.

If there is something in you that says where you are right now is not how the story is supposed to end, then this study will be important for you. If your heart tells you there is something more to your life than the tasks on your to-do list, then these seven weeks will be well spent.

God is the author of the greatest story. God is the main character, but you have a role to play.

## How to Use These Devotions

**Be Still:** It is recommended that you set aside a certain time and place each day to do your *God Story* devotion. Find a place where you can sit comfortably, but not so comfortable that you fall asleep! Once you are seated take a deep breath. Let the thoughts and worries of your day fade out of your mind. Don't rush the beginning of your time with God. Be still and allow your heart to open to God.

**Pray:** Once you have found a still place, you will begin with the simple prayer for the week found on the title page for each week. Read the prayer silently or aloud. The same prayer will be said each day of the week at the beginning and the end of your devotion time. This repetition will allow the theme for the week to sink into your heart and be carried with you throughout the day.

**Read:** Next is a selected passage of Scripture. The Scripture for the week is found on the title page for the week. Read the Scripture in its entirety.

**Focus:** Each day there will be a focus verse: a shorter passage for you to focus on for the day.

**Read:** Then you will find the devotional thought for each day. Read the reflection and consider how this Scripture intersects with your life today.

**Write:** Each day you will find reflection questions where you can write your thoughts or questions.

**Pray:** You are invited again to pray the prayer for that week.

---

1. G.K. Chesterton, *Orthodoxy* (Scotts Valley, CA: IAP, 2009), 39.

# Week 1:
# Introduction

*O God, thank you for writing me into your story. I find purpose in knowing that I am a part of the greatest story of all. Even if I am faced with uncertainty today help me to see how I am connected to you. I believe you are a God who still speaks, help me to hear your voice today. In Jesus' name. Amen.*

## Genesis 1:1-2, 26—2:4

When God began to create the heavens and the earth—the earth was without shape or form, it was dark over the deep sea, and God's wind swept over the waters. . . .

Then God said, "Let us make humanity in our image to resemble us so that they may take charge of the fish of the sea, the birds of the sky, the livestock, all the earth, and all the crawling things on earth."

God created humanity in God's own image,
in the divine image God created them,
male and female God created them.

God blessed them and said to them, "Be fertile and multiply;
fill the earth and master it. Take charge of the fish of the sea,
the birds of the sky, and everything crawling on the ground."
Then God said, "I now give to you all the plants on the earth
that yield seeds and all the trees whose fruit produces its
seeds within it. These will be your food. To all wildlife, to
all the birds of the sky, and to everything crawling on the
ground—to everything that breathes—I give all the green
grasses for food." And that's what happened. God saw everything he had made: it was supremely good.

There was evening and there was morning: the sixth day.

The heavens and the earth and all who live in them were
completed. On the sixth day God completed all the work that
he had done, and on the seventh day God rested from all
the work that he had done. God blessed the seventh day and
made it holy, because on it God rested from all the work of
creation. This is the account of the heavens and the earth
when they were created.

# Day 1

We all have a story. You know the chapters and the characters in your story. You know the moments of heartbreak and the moments of glory.

How often do you think that your life is not just a haphazard collection of events but that your story is a part of God's story, which means your life has purpose and meaning?

It is easy to get caught up in the day-to-day and not think about the greater purpose for our story.

G.K. Chesterton said, "I had always felt life first as a story: and if there is a story there is a story-teller."[1]

David said of God:

> You are the one who created my innermost parts;
>> you knit me together while I was still in my mother's womb.
>>>> Psalm 139:13

David was recognizing that it was God who created all things in the beginning and who created him in the beginning. If we recognize God as author of our story, how should we live differently?

As we began this study of the God Story, first consider what has already come in your life.

If you had to divide your life into chapters up to this point, what would you title them?

Chapter 1:_____

Chapter 2:_____

Chapter 3:_____

Chapter 4:_____

What's next?

Chapter 5:_____

As you look back on your story and the possibilities of the future, what do you feel led to give thanks for today?


*O God, thank you for writing me into your story. I find purpose in knowing that I am a part of the greatest story of all. Even if I am faced with uncertainty today help me to see how I am connected to you. I believe you are a God who still speaks, help me to hear your voice today. In Jesus' name. Amen.*

_____

1. G.K. Chesterton, *Orthodoxy* (Scotts Valley, CA: IAP, 2009), 39.

# Day 2

I often wish I had been given a blueprint at the beginning of my life—a map of sorts that told me where I was supposed to go and when.

Life, though, does not follow a simple formula. Instead we experience life like a story. We turn the next page and see what is there. Sometimes it is what we expected. Usually it is something we didn't.

Life is a drama, an adventure, sometimes a comedy, sometimes a tragedy, but always a story.

It unfolds whether we want it to or not, sometimes too fast, sometimes too slow.

As a child, I often pretended I was in a suspenseful adventure. In make believe times, I was the hero who encountered love, heartbreak, and the unknown. As an adult, I no longer have to pretend these things. Life is an adventure with love, heartbreak, and the unknown.

Part of living in the middle of a story means that you can't skip ahead and see the last chapter to see how this thing ends.

This can lead to wondering what in the world God is up to.

I don't get it. How does it all fit together?

David often asked this of God in the Psalms. Here is his heart in Psalm 13:

> How long, O LORD? Will you forget me forever?
>> How long will you hide your face from me?
>>>> Psalm 13:1 (NRSV)

Clearly David was having some trouble seeing where he fit into God's story, if he fit at all.

We have a God who can handle our questions. We don't always get immediate clarity, but there is power in the questioning. Is there anything you would like to ask God today?

*O God, thank you for writing me into your story. I find purpose in knowing that I am a part of the greatest story of all. Even if I am faced with uncertainty today help me to see how I am connected to you. I believe you are a God who still speaks, help me to hear your voice today. In Jesus' name. Amen.*

# Day 3

The Bible is a big book. In fact it is a collection of sixty-six smaller books. They were written by different people in different times in different circumstances.

If you are like me, you can look at the Bible, this big book, and hear the names Adam and Eve, Noah, Abraham and Sarah, Joseph, David, Mary, Jesus and wonder how they all fit together. Is this one story or a hundred stories? Does the God of Adam have anything to do with the God of Abraham, and what do they have to do with Jesus?

And then of course . . . what does it have to do with me?

Amazingly, the Bible has threads that run throughout it connecting the characters with each other and with God. Over the next several weeks we will uncover these threads to see how the God Story is connected.

We will see that the Bible is not a haphazard collection of cute bedtime stories, but the Word of God speaking to us a connected story of hope for our lives. The longings that are expressed in the imaginations of eight-year-olds and the empty longings of fifty-year-olds find their resolution in this great story.

If you lack clarity about the story or where you fit in, know today that is a good starting place for you. If you feel empty as it relates to your purpose in life, know that is a good starting place.

> Now the earth was formless and empty,
>> darkness was over the surface of the deep...
>>> Genesis 1:2*a* (NIV)

God began the story "in the beginning" with nothingness and void. Things were cloudy and dark. But God didn't leave it that way.

> ...and the Spirit of God was hovering over the waters.
>> Genesis 1:2*b* (NIV)

God was present above and with the emptiness and darkness.

Where are you experiencing emptiness and darkness?

God is present with you.

*O God, thank you for writing me into your story. I find purpose in knowing that I am a part of the greatest story of all. Even if I am faced with uncertainty today help me to see how I am connected to you. I believe you are a God who still speaks, help me to hear your voice today. In Jesus' name. Amen.*

# Day 4

Where does any good story start?

"Once upon a time…"

"A long time ago in a galaxy far, far away…"

"In the beginning."

That's where our story starts, right where any good story starts: at the beginning.

> In the beginning God created the heavens
>    and the earth.
>
> Genesis 1:1 (NIV)

And right there in the beginning God gets the whole thing started by speaking. God speaks things into existence.

Light, sky, land, trees, plants, stars, sun, moon, creatures in the water, creatures on the land, and then us.

Many people look at Genesis to learn about Creation, the age of the world, science, etc. The best thing that Genesis has to tell us, though, is about God. One purpose of the Introduction of a good story is to introduce the main character. In the God Story, the main character is, well, God.

Over the next three days we will look at three things that the Introduction to the God Story in Genesis tells us about God. The first is this: God is extremely powerful. God is the only being that can create out of nothing. As we journey through the God Story we will be amazed at how God relates to God's creation. Yet, don't miss this first. God is God. And God is full of power.

God has power to create and power for your life.

Where do you need God's power in your life? Where do you need something that only God can do?

*O God, thank you for writing me into your story. I find purpose in knowing that I am a part of the greatest story of all. Even if I am faced with uncertainty today help me to see how I am connected to you. I believe you are a God who still speaks, help me to hear your voice today. In Jesus' name. Amen.*

# Day 5

Sometimes I catch a glimpse of my oldest daughter and for a moment I feel I am looking at myself about 25 years ago. She looks like me. I look like her. I'm sure there will be times she wishes that she looked more like her mother. I hope there are many other times that her resemblance to me causes her joy to know that she is my child.

> God created humanity in God's own image,
>     in the divine image God created them.
>
> Genesis 1:27*a*

We were created like God. We resemble God. Even on our worst days we carry the image of God.

So often we focus on the frailty that comes with our humanity. We so easily see our weakness and fragility. We seem to get daily reminders of our propensity to mess up. In Creation God created us in the image of God so that we would not forget that of the eternal that is in us.

God, the great Storyteller, is powerful, creative, and imaginative. God the great Storyteller made us like God, so we get to join the powerful, creative, imaginative things God is doing.

So we are not just a part of a great story; we get to be storytellers ourselves. We create things and dream dreams.

What does it mean to you today to know that you were created in the image of God?

What story is God calling you to write? What does God want you to create?

How can you resemble God today?

*O God, thank you for writing me into your story. I find purpose in knowing that I am a part of the greatest story of all. Even if I am faced with uncertainty today help me to see how I am connected to you. I believe you are a God who still speaks, help me to hear your voice today. In Jesus' name. Amen.*

# Day 6

After God creates humanity, God does something peculiar. God speaks.

God speaks to that which God created. God does not desire to be a far-off God. God does not create, set this world in motion, and then step away. God speaks.

Why?

*God speaks because God desires relationship with us.* This will be Thread #1 in the God Story. We will see it over and over in the God Story. Our God is not like other gods. Our God speaks, initiates conversation with us, and the conversation leads to continued relationship.

Is your heart open today to hear the voice of God whispering, maybe speaking, perhaps even shouting to you of your connection to the story?

I have an old friend who, every time I think he has forgotten about me, will, at the right time, send a text, make a call, or show up at my house. Why does he do it? He desires our relationship to continue.

There are times in the God Story when we think God has gone silent for good. This is not the case. We must hang in there.

We must continue to speak and continue to listen.

God has something to say to you today.

Be still and listen for a moment.

What do you think God wants to say to you?

What do you need to say to God?

*O God, thank you for writing me into your story. I find pur-pose in knowing that I am a part of the greatest story of all. Even if I am faced with uncertainty today help me to see how I am connected to you. I believe you are a God who still speaks, help me to hear your voice today. In Jesus' name. Amen.*

# Day 7

There is a longing in all of us to be a part of the God Story. I think it begins in the imagination and fairy tales of childhood. As children, we dream of greatness, we see ourselves as heroes and heroines in a bigger story.

The longings of your child-like heart for adventure and relationship for adventure and love are not to be dismissed. They are the echo of the greatest story that has ever been told bouncing off of your heart. It is the thread of God's desire for you pulling you back into the story.

Frederick Buechner wrote that God is "indeed speaking to us, and that, however little we may understand of it, his word to each of us is both recoverable and precious beyond telling."[1]

Over time our hearts can become hardened.

Our hearts get broken.

If your heart is hard or broken today or if it has been a long while since you heard God calling to your heart, know that God's word to you is recoverable and worth recovering.

God still has a dream for you, a dream for greatness where you get a role in the great story. Don't give up on that. Don't give up on what God has for you.

Remember God speaks to you because God desires relationship with you.

What does it mean to you today to know that God desires you to be a part of the God Story? That God desires to be in relationship with you?

*O God, thank you for writing me into your story. I find purpose in knowing that I am a part of the greatest story of all. Even if I am faced with uncertainty today help me to see how I am connected to you. I believe you are a God who still speaks, help me to hear your voice today. In Jesus' name. Amen.*

---

1. Frederick Buechner, *Now and Then: A Memoir of Vocation* (San Francisco: HarperCollins, 1983), 3.

# Week 2:
## Suspension of Disbelief

*God, I want to fully live into the story you have for my life. Give me faith today to trust in you in the places in my life where I still can't see what you are up to. I believe; help my unbelief. Amen.*

## Genesis 18:1-15

The LORD appeared to Abraham at the oaks of Mamre while he sat at the entrance of his tent in the day's heat. He looked up and suddenly saw three men standing near him. As soon as he saw them, he ran from his tent entrance to greet them and bowed deeply. He said, "Sirs, if you would be so kind, don't just pass by your servant. Let a little water be brought so you may wash your feet and refresh yourselves under the tree. Let me offer you a little bread so you will feel stronger, and after that you may leave your servant and go on your way—since you have visited your servant."

They responded, "Fine. Do just as you have said."

So Abraham hurried to Sarah at his tent and said, "Hurry! Knead three seahs of the finest flour and make some baked goods!" Abraham ran to the cattle, took a healthy young calf, and gave it to a young servant, who prepared it quickly. Then Abraham took butter, milk, and the calf that had been prepared, put the food in front of them, and stood under the tree near them as they ate.

They said to him, "Where's your wife Sarah?

And he said, "Right here in the tent."

Then one of the men said, "I will definitely return to you about this time next year. Then your wife Sarah will have a son!"

Sarah was listening at the tent door behind him. Now Abraham and Sarah were both very old. Sarah was no longer menstruating. So Sarah laughed to herself, thinking, I'm no longer able to have children and my husband's old.

The Lord said to Abraham, "Why did Sarah laugh and say, 'Me give birth? At my age?' Is anything too difficult for the Lord? When I return to you about this time next year, Sarah will have a son."

Sarah lied and said, "I didn't laugh," because she was frightened.

But he said, "No, you laughed."

# Day 1

God asks us to believe the unbelievable.

In literature, this is called suspending disbelief. The concept of the "willing suspension of disbelief" was first introduced by the English poet Samuel Taylor Coleridge in 1817. He said that when reading fantastic or non-realistic elements of literature there is a Suspension of Disbelief that is required. In other words, you have to be willing to suspend your tendency not to believe the impossible to have any hope of enjoying the story.[1]

If you think of many of your favorite stories you will realize that a Suspension of Disbelief is necessary. We put reason and logic aside to enter into the story.

If you are going to enjoy the Superman story, then you have to believe that when Superman dons the dorky glasses and opens his eyes wide that no one can tell Clark Kent is Superman. If you are not willing to do that, you might as well move on. But we do it because the story is so good. We Suspend our Disbelief and enjoy the story.

> Faith is the reality of what we hope for, the proof of what we don't see.
>
> Hebrews 11:1

God asks us to believe some things that at first glance seem unbelievable. God calls upon us to have faith which is the proof of what we don't see.

If we base our lives only on what our eyes can see, we will miss out on some of the best parts of the story.

God is inviting you to play a role in the God Story. It will require you to suspend your disbelief and simply believe.

What are you hoping for in your story?

*God, I want to fully live into the story you have for my life. Give me faith today to trust in you in the places in my life where I still can't see what you are up to. I believe; help my unbelief. Amen.*

---

1. Coleridge expounded on his groundbreaking literary concept, the "willing suspension of disbelief," in his well-known autobiography *Biographia Literaria; Or Biographical Sketches of My Literary Life and Opinions* (Princeton: Princeton University Press, 1983).

# Day 2

The improbable story of Rudy Ruettiger has captivated people now for decades. Rudy was the third of fourteen children of a lower class family. He had undiagnosed dyslexia. He was 5 feet 6 inches tall. He walked on to the Notre Dame football team.

In the final game of his final season, on the final play his coach sent him into the game and he sacked the quarterback. His teammates put him on their shoulders and marched him around the field. It is an amazing story that requires the Suspension of Disbelief. Who would believe this improbable story?

But there's one important thing to note about Rudy's story: it's true.[1]

Keep in mind, as we talk about the fantastic story of God and God's people, that it is true. It will require great faith and certainly the Suspension of Disbelief, but please understand, fantasy does not necessarily mean fiction.

The God Story is amazingly improbable and amazingly true.

There will be times in your true story when you will be forced to have great faith in a God who is calling you to the seemingly impossible. These will be some of the most important moments of your story. You will need to suspend your disbelief so you can be caught up in the amazing, surprising next chapter that God holds for you.

Once there was a man who brought his son to Jesus for healing (Mark 9:14-29). The son was plagued by a spirit that caused him great anguish and distress. The man asked Jesus, "If you can do anything, please help us!"

Jesus responded, "If I can do anything? All things are possible for the one who has faith." The father responds, "I believe, help my unbelief."

You may feel that way. There are parts of me that believe, parts of me that want to believe. But, if I am honest there are parts of me that don't. Our finite minds don't grasp the depth of God's power and majesty. We just don't understand fully.

The father's honest response lead him to suspending his disbelief and opening himself up to the unbelievable things that only God can do.

What are you having trouble believing? Where do you need help with your unbelief?

*God, I want to fully live into the story you have for my life. Give me faith today to trust in you in the places in my life where I still can't see what you are up to. I believe; help my unbelief. Amen.*

---

1. Ruettiger's story is portrayed in the 1993 TriStar Pictures film *Rudy*.

# Day 3

Some of us wait a long time to figure out where we fit in the God Story.

Abram was seventy-five when he heard God speaking to him. Abram, he thought, was on the downhill portion of his part of the story. Some of the things he had hoped would happen happened, but many had not.

At age seventy-five Abram heard God speak:

> The LORD said to Abram, "Leave your land, your family, and your father's household for the land that I will show you. I will make of you a great nation and will bless you. I will make your name respected, and you will be a blessing."
>
> Genesis 12:1-2

Pretty cool if you get this word at age eighteen, but at seventy-five this had to seem nothing short of impossible. God is going to make Abram's name great at seventy-five? God seems a little late to the party.

And this part about making Abram a great nation implies that Abram and Sarah's offspring will multiply and multiply. Abram's sons and daughters will make his name great. Trouble is, Abram has no sons and daughters. He is, may I remind you, seventy-five years old.

Abram is a key character in the story of God's people. Hundreds of times God would in fact be referred to as the God of Abraham. So what was it that made Abram so significant?

Well, after God gave him this improbable promise the Bible says, "Abram left just as the LORD told him" (Genesis 12:4).

Abram wasn't highly qualified; he wasn't especially special. He shouldn't have been the prime candidate to start a family. But he was willing to go where God sent him. He was willing to believe the unbelievable.

What are the things that should disqualify you from being used by God?

These obstacles are easily overcome by God, and it is God that is writing your story.

*God, I want to fully live into the story you have for my life. Give me faith today to trust in you in the places in my life where I still can't see what you are up to. I believe; help my unbelief. Amen.*

# Day 4

After God's initial promise to Abram, God continues to speak to him. God's message is the same.

> "Don't be afraid, Abram. I am your protector. Your reward will be very great."
>
> Genesis 15:1

Abram at this point can see the cold hard facts that are before him. He is an old man, with no children, and there is no way that he is going to be the father of many nations.

He brings this up to God.

God's response?

God takes Abram outside, points his eyes to the sky, and says, "Look up at the sky and count the stars if you think you can count them. This is how many children you will have" (Genesis 15:5).

God still believes in the promise and so Abram does too.

God changes Abram's name to Abraham, which means father of many. At the age of ninety-nine, Abraham falls facedown and laughs. Sarah hears the message too and she laughs.

What is God up to here? What is God setting up?

Could it be that God wants us to believe that the laughable dreams of our hearts might still be possible? But, they will only be possible through God's power. So all the circumstances that could lead us to believe that we are in control or that we can determine the outcome are taken away.

Do you find yourself in a place now where your dreams would be considered laughable? If so, ask yourself what have you yet to relinquish to God's power?

What would it mean for you to trust in God to do the impossible?

*God, I want to fully live into the story you have for my life. Give me faith today to trust in you in the places in my life where I still can't see what you are up to. I believe; help my unbelief. Amen.*

# Day 5

People often let us down. They don't keep their word; they don't follow through; they over-promise and under-deliver. So, naturally we can become a little reluctant when it comes to trusting people.

Many times we bring our reluctance to trust into our relationship with God. We don't mean to; it's just that we have conditioned ourselves to be guarded and hesitant in other relationships, and it is hard to flip the switch with God and believe the promises of God.

God made incredible promises to Abraham and we have marveled at his faith, but we have also seen his reluctance and hesitancy to believe the miraculous. Abraham and Sarah laughed at God's promise to them.

Over and over again we see the thread of God's trustworthiness in the Scriptures. Thread #2: *If God makes a promise, it will come true.*

The prophet Isaiah speaks these words of God:

> so is my word that goes out from my mouth:
> It will not return to me empty,
> but will accomplish what I desire
> and achieve the purpose for which I sent it.
> Isaiah 55:11 (NIV)

This doesn't mean it always happens in our timing or the way that we would have desired. But, God's word will always achieve the purpose for which God sent it. Trusting in this thread may mean a change in thinking for you. If you have become conditioned by the world and human relationships to be mistrusting then it may be difficult for you to step into God's promises.

We should not judge God's character on that which we have seen in people. We trust in God because God is trustworthy!

How do you think some of your human relationships have affected the way you think about God?

Where do you need to trust God today? What do you need to trust God for?

*God, I want to fully live into the story you have for my life. Give me faith today to trust in you in the places in my life where I still can't see what you are up to. I believe; help my unbelief. Amen.*

# Day 6

God asked Abraham this question:

"Is anything too difficult for the LORD?"

Genesis 18:14 (NIV)

No doubt, there are some difficult things facing you. There are some parts of your story that you didn't expect. There may be some things about today that you have no idea which way they will go.

God asks you too,

*"Is anything too difficult for the Lord?"*

As we look at the mountains in our life we can easily say that they are too big for us. We can't handle it. We have no solution.

But, as people who believe in the God of Abraham, we know that there is nothing too big for our God. There is nothing too difficult for the Lord who fulfilled his promise to an old man and old woman who thought that their story was nearing its end.

Is there something in your life that seems too difficult for the Lord?

Place that something in the blank below.

*Is _____ too difficult for the Lord?*

Now bring that something before God in prayer. Entrust it to God. Hand it over to God.

Nothing is too difficult for the God of Abraham.

*God, I want to fully live into the story you have for my life. Give me faith today to trust in you in the places in my life where I still can't see what you are up to. I believe; help my unbelief. Amen.*

# Day 7

In Paul's great letter to the Romans he reflected on Abraham's story of faith and God's unwavering trustworthy nature:

> Therefore, the promise comes by faith, so that it may be grace and may be guaranteed to all Abraham's offspring—not only to those who are of the law but also to those who have the faith of Abraham.
>
> Romans 4:16 (NIV)

Who is Paul talking about? He continues…

*Us! We are a part of the story! He is the father of us all.*

Abraham's story is not just an ancient tale in a historic book. His story is our story. God told Abraham he would be the father of many nations. Sure, he was staring his one-hundredth birthday in the eyes when the promise was made, but Abraham believed and God kept the promise.

You are a part of Abraham's legacy of faith. You are his heritage today. We are the extension of the promise God made through Abraham.

> He is our father in the sight of God, in whom he believed—the God who gives life to the dead and calls into being things that were not.
>
> Romans 4:17b (NIV)

This is not a cute bedtime story; this is the story that leads to Jesus that leads to life. The story God has written you into is one of life. Life for you, life for all. Nothing is too difficult for our God, the one who gives life to the dead and calls things that are not as though they were.

The dreams that lie dormant in your heart, the ones that you thought were not, might still be a part of your story. Not because you are clever or talented enough to make them happen, but because you believe in a God who calls things that are not as though they were.

God's story is a story where laughable dreams come true.

God's story is a story of life.

It is your story.

Imagine yourself as one of the stars Abraham saw that night. What does it mean to you to be part of that same story of faith?

*God, I want to fully live into the story you have for my life. Give me faith today to trust in you in the places in my life where I still can't see what you are up to. I believe; help my unbelief. Amen.*

# Week 3: Rising Action

*God, if I have any hope of leaving behind hurtful things in my past it will be because you deliver me. Thank you that you are a God who delivers us out of slavery and leads us to freedom. Give me the strength needed to walk the journey toward the Promised Land that you have for me. When I get weary, uphold me, when I lose focus, give me clarity, when I want to give up, give me hope. In Jesus' name. Amen.*

## Exodus 16:2-4, 13-16

The whole Israelite community complained against Moses and Aaron in the desert. The Israelites said to them, "Oh, how we wish that the LORD had just put us to death while we were still in the land of Egypt. There we could sit by the pots cooking meat and eat our fill of bread. Instead, you've brought us out into this desert to starve this whole assembly to death."

Then the LORD said to Moses, "I'm going to make bread rain down from the sky for you. The people will go out each day and gather just enough for that day. In this way, I'll test them to see whether or not they follow my Instruction.

In the evening a flock of quail flew down and covered the camp. And in the morning there was a layer of dew all around the camp. When the layer of dew lifted, there on the desert surface were thin flakes, as thin as frost on the ground. When the Israelites saw it, they said to each other, "What is it?" They didn't know what it was.

Moses said to them, "This is the bread that the LORD has given you to eat. This is what the LORD has commanded: 'Collect as much of it as each of you can eat, one omer per person. You may collect for the number of people in your household.'"

## Numbers 11:4-6

The riffraff among them had a strong craving. Even the Israelites cried again and said, "Who will give us meat to eat? We remember the fish we ate in Egypt for free, the cucumbers, the melons, the leeks, the onions, and the garlic. Now our lives are wasting away. There is nothing but manna in front of us."

# Day 1

What we find in the Book of Exodus is the record of a people who were enslaved, who then became a people on the run, who then became a people with no home. The Exodus story is a transition story, a deliverance story, and it is an independence story.

Though the details would be different, the Exodus story would not be unlike the story of an African people who became enslaved in a faraway country and then worked for and found freedom.

Both stories have an initial groundbreaking event of freedom being found, but the event does not signal the end of the suffering, hardship, and oppression of the people. Those cycles take decades, if not centuries, to move through.

The Exodus portion of the God Story is of great importance. It signals the end to a time of great pain, giving hope for a great future, but that future is still far off.

Most likely you find yourself in some type of transition right now. Life is one transition to the next. As we begin this week looking at the Exodus it may be helpful for you to think about that which you have left behind or hope to leave behind, and the new land that you are hoping to enter.

As you consider your story, what time(s) would you consider to have been Egypt times? (times of pain, suffering, hurtful relationships)

You may be in one of those places now. Take heart in knowing that we have a God that releases people from bondage and desires that for you.

As you consider your story, what would be the Promised Land for you? Where do you hope you are going?

You probably aren't there yet. Take heart in knowing that we have a God who travels the journey with us.

*God, if I have any hope of leaving behind hurtful things in my past it will be because you deliver me. Thank you that you are a God who delivers us out of slavery and leads us to freedom. Give me the strength needed to walk the journey toward the Promised Land that you have for me. When I get weary, uphold me, when I lose focus, give me clarity, when I want to give up, give me hope. In Jesus' name. Amen.*

# Day 2

If the Bible is one grand story then Exodus is one of the places of Rising Action. You may remember the elements of story from your Literature class in middle school. If not, I'll refresh you: the Rising Action occurs when the basic conflict of the story is complicated by the introduction of secondary conflicts including various obstacles that frustrate the main character's attempt to reach his or her goal.

The basic conflict of the God Story is our separation from God. It started in the garden and runs throughout the whole story. We see the Rising Action in Exodus because secondary problems like slavery, hunger, and exhaustion further complicate the already growing issue of a nation of people trying to stay connected with God.

The God Story, of course, does not fit perfectly in the middle school diagram of elements of story. Neither does your life. However, I'm sure you can see times when it seems there is more than just one problem in your life, and your ability to stay focused on your goals is getting increasingly difficult.

Rarely do we get overwhelmed in life when there is just one thing going on. It is when secondary conflicts and various obstacles begin to mount that we grow frustrated.

Moses found himself in this place. He knew God had something good for him in the future, but there was so much noise from the problems in his life he was having trouble hearing God's voice.

At one point Moses is so frustrated that he tells God that as far as he is concerned if this is how it's going to be then God can end the whole thing. It is at this point that I believe Moses began to listen more to the voice of the problems than to the voice of God. God had given steady reminders along the way of his presence and provision, but Moses could only see the obstacles.

This is why it is important to stop daily and be reminded of God's presence with you on the journey.

What things can you see today that remind you God is with you?

As you reflect on these reminders allow your heart to be comforted by the promise of God's presence. Carry this presence with you throughout the day seeking to hear God's voice above the noise of your problems.

*God, if I have any hope of leaving behind hurtful things in my past it will be because you deliver me. Thank you that you are a God who delivers us out of slavery and leads us to freedom. Give me the strength needed to walk the journey toward the Promised Land that you have for me. When I get weary, uphold me, when I lose focus, give me clarity, when I want to give up, give me hope. In Jesus' name. Amen.*

# Day 3

Out in the desert, things started to get ugly.

The people were hungry and mad. Mad and hungry. Not a good combination. And when you are mad you usually focus it on someone. Lucky Moses. They accused Moses of bringing them out into the wilderness to starve.

Starving in the wilderness, though, was not what God had promised so it was not what God would do.

> Then the LORD said to Moses, "I'm going to make bread rain down from the sky for you. The people will go out each day and gather just enough for that day."
>
> Exodus 16:4

Thread #3 that we see in the God Story is found in God's raining bread from heaven on the hungry people in the desert.

Thread #3: *God will provide all you need for the journey.*

Notice what God provided for the Israelites. God gave enough bread for the day. They could gather just enough for that day. They couldn't store it up. They couldn't save some for retirement. They had bread for the day.

When Jesus' followers asked him how to pray, he included a request for "daily bread." I have to think he was referring to our spiritual ancestors who were given what they needed for the day.

This is difficult for us because we want the assurance not just of needs being met today, but we would like to know that tomorrow is going to be ok, and the next day too if we can.

Trusting God, though, often involves placing the future in God's hands and taking hold of what God has for us today.

Why do you think God gave bread for only one day?

How do you think the concept of "daily bread" might apply to your life?

*God, if I have any hope of leaving behind hurtful things in my past it will be because you deliver me. Thank you that you are a God who delivers us out of slavery and leads us to freedom. Give me the strength needed to walk the journey toward the Promised Land that you have for me. When I get weary, uphold me, when I lose focus, give me clarity, when I want to give up, give me hope. In Jesus' name. Amen.*

# Day 4

As the Israelites continued their long journey toward the Promised Land a murmur began to grow among the people. I imagine a scene one night around the campfire as the people rested after a long day of wandering.

Somebody says, "Hey, remember when we were back in Egypt?" Another knows exactly where he's headed and interjects, "Yeah, we had meat to eat."

A long silence.

And then another says, "yeah and cucumbers." And then they all join in as they share all the things that they had in Egypt that they don't have now.

Then finally someone says what they had all been thinking but no one had the courage to say.

"Why don't we just go back?"

There will come moments in transition times even after the initial release from slavery when we will be tempted to go back. Have you ever heard someone say, "I will never go back to that restaurant again?" You know they have had such a bad experience that they promise never to step foot in that establishment again.

My experience with these types of statements is that you usually find yourself for one reason or another being tempted to go back. It sounds crazy, but over time the memory of the reasons for your promise begin to fade and you find yourself heading back to where you said you would never return.

The people of God who had been delivered from slavery, given water in the desert, bread from heaven, after a little while wandering say, "Let's just go back."

The Exodus story is a warning to us that our journey can get long too. We can lose some of the initial excitement and energy we had when we first began to follow God. We may even be tempted to go back.

It is at these times that we must choose not to join in the back-to-Egypt conversations. Are you currently involved in any conversations that are leading you further away from the Promised Land rather than closer to it?

Choose today to go with God even in times when the road is difficult.

*God, if I have any hope of leaving behind hurtful things in my past it will be because you deliver me. Thank you that you are a God who delivers us out of slavery and leads us to freedom. Give me the strength needed to walk the journey toward the Promised Land that you have for me. When I get weary, uphold me, when I lose focus, give me clarity, when I want to give up, give me hope. In Jesus' name. Amen.*

# Day 5

A re you in a chapter of transition?

Are you in between jobs, moving towards a new life stage, or simply hoping the next page will turn?

You may very well be in a chapter of transition, which can mean that you are in a chapter of deliverance. We learn from the Exodus story there are some things we should be wary of when we find ourselves in transition.

Transition times are one of those strange times when things seem to be moving very slow and very fast at the same time. It feels slow in that you wonder when it will ever end. It moves fast in that it is hard to take stock of everything that is going on.

We learn from the Israelites that this slow/fast transition time is an easy time to become distracted. It is also an easy time to become exhausted.

As you grow increasingly distracted and exhausted you become vulnerable, vulnerable to turn around and to turn away from where God is sending you.

Surely if the Israelites thought about it real hard they would not have preferred to live in Egypt again. It was a place of slavery and abuse. Life in the desert, though, is a transition time that crawls by and goes fast at the same time and you rarely stop to realize where you are and where you are really going. You can easily become distracted by those things that frustrate you about the journey and seek quick relief. You can easily become exhausted which leads to complaining, grumbling, and unhealthy desires.

God does have good things in store for you! Your story has purpose. So it could be helpful today to take stock of a few things.

Where are you and where do you think God is leading you?

What is it that easily distracts you?

Are you rested today or exhausted? If exhausted, how can you find rest today?

*God, if I have any hope of leaving behind hurtful things in my past it will be because you deliver me. Thank you that you are a God who delivers us out of slavery and leads us to freedom. Give me the strength needed to walk the journey toward the Promised Land that you have for me. When I get weary, uphold me, when I lose focus, give me clarity, when I want to give up, give me hope. In Jesus' name. Amen.*

# Day 6

God does some of God's best work on the journey.

The transition times, the Rising Actions, are in many ways the best part of the story. It is here that your character is formed.

We have talked about how there is inevitably suffering experienced and endured on the journey. Paul says that with God, suffering can be a great catalyst to good things in your life.

> Suffering produces perseverance.
> Perseverance leads to character.
> Character builds hope.
>
> Romans 5:3-4 (NIV paraphrase)

It is not the "in the beginning" or the "happily ever after" that defines you. It is the progression of suffering to hope that forms who we truly are. It is on the journey that we become who we were made to be. In suffering we learn perseverance, as we persevere our character is formed, and a person of character finds hope in Christ.

The Hebrew people would re-tell one story over and over again. It was the story of their Exodus. They told it every year to remind them what they went through and to remind them of their great God. God took care of them then, and God will take care of them now.

They re-told the story just like any group that has been delivered re-tells their independence story, so they will not go back.

It is possible that the very things you are enduring today will
produce in you a perseverance that builds your character and
gives you hope.

Write the things that are causing you suffering today:

It is important to note these things and remember that God will
provide all you need for this part of the journey. God travels
with you. God will never leave you. Let that be your hope today.

*God, if I have any hope of leaving behind hurtful things in
my past it will be because you deliver me. Thank you that you
are a God who delivers us out of slavery and leads us to freedom. Give me the strength needed to walk the journey toward
the Promised Land that you have for me. When I get weary,
uphold me, when I lose focus, give me clarity, when I want to
give up, give me hope. In Jesus' name. Amen.*

# Day 7

You know that feeling of being really hungry? Your stomach aches and your head begins to swim.

The Israelites in the wilderness were hungry. God sent bread from heaven.

Imagine what it must have been like that first morning. After a night of hearing tummies rumbling in their tents they awake to find the ground covered like snow...with bread.

For the Israelites this manna was a tangible reminder of Thread #3 in God's Story. *God will provide all we need for the journey.*

Many hundreds of years after their ancestors received the manna from heaven, the Hebrew people found themselves again waiting. Waiting for deliverance, for independence, for a new life.

Some of them heard the teachings of a new rabbi who taught with an authority that grabbed their attention. His name was Jesus (John 6).

They asked him for a sign, a miracle. They reminded him of what God had done for their ancestors, and asked, "Where is our bread from heaven?"

Jesus said, "I am the bread."

When Jesus made the strange pronouncement that he was their bread, he was of course saying to them: "I am the sign. I am the miracle. I am the tangible reminder to you that God will provide all you need for the journey."

Jesus was saying, "I am all you need for the journey."

We find Jesus when we're at our hungriest. He hears our bellies aching for something more. He knows our heads hurt under the pressure of all we face.

Jesus wants you to cling to him in this season of your life. He will walk through the transition with you.

Are you hungering for him?

What does it mean to you to know that "Jesus is the bread of life" (John 6:35)?

*God, if I have any hope of leaving behind hurtful things in my past it will be because you deliver me. Thank you that you are a God who delivers us out of slavery and leads us to freedom. Give me the strength needed to walk the journey toward the Promised Land that you have for me. When I get weary, uphold me, when I lose focus, give me clarity, when I want to give up, give me hope. In Jesus' name. Amen.*

# Week 4: The Inciting Incident

*God, thank you for being present with me at all times. You have been with me in every life-changing moment, and I know you are here with me today. Help me to look for you in my story. Help me to hear how you are calling me into your story. In Jesus' name. Amen.*

## 1 Samuel 16:1-13

The LORD said to Samuel, "How long are you going to grieve over Saul? I have rejected him as king over Israel. Fill your horn with oil and get going. I'm sending you to Jesse of Bethlehem because I have found my next king among his sons."

"How can I do that?" Samuel asked. "When Saul hears of it he'll kill me!"

"Take a heifer with you," the LORD replied, "and say, 'I have come to make a sacrifice to the LORD.' Invite Jesse to the sacrifice, and I will make clear to you what you should do. You will anoint for me the person I point out to you."

Samuel did what the LORD instructed. When he came to Bethlehem, the city elders came to meet him. They were shaking with fear. "Do you come in peace?" they asked.

"Yes," Samuel answered. "I've come to make a sacrifice to the LORD. Now make yourselves holy, then come with me to the sacrifice." Samuel made Jesse and his sons holy and invited them to the sacrifice as well.

When they arrived, Samuel looked at Eliab and thought, That must be the LORD's anointed right in front.

But the LORD said to Samuel, "Have no regard for his appearance or stature, because I haven't selected him. God doesn't look at things like humans do. Humans see only what is visible to the eyes, but the LORD sees into the heart."

Next Jesse called for Abinadab, who presented himself to Samuel, but he said, "The LORD hasn't chosen this one either." So Jesse presented Shammah, but Samuel said, "No, the LORD hasn't chosen this one." Jesse presented seven of his sons to Samuel, but Samuel said to Jesse, "The LORD hasn't picked any of these." Then Samuel asked Jesse, "Is that all of your boys?"

"There is still the youngest one," Jesse answered, "but he's out keeping the sheep."

"Send for him," Samuel told Jesse, "because we can't proceed until he gets here."

So Jesse sent and brought him in. He was reddish brown, had beautiful eyes, and was good-looking. The LORD said, "That's the one. Go anoint him." So Samuel took the horn of oil and anointed him right there in front of his brothers. The LORD's spirit came over David from that point forward. Then Samuel left and went to Ramah.

# Day 1

From time to time Jesus would quote Scripture as a way of teaching others.

Sometimes he would share about God in a way that people would later call a sermon.

Many times, though, when Jesus wanted to share a hard to explain spiritual truth he didn't preach a sermon or quote Scripture.

He would tell a story.

Jesus would tell a story that the people could understand.

Jesus knew most people would connect with a story in a way that they wouldn't with dogmatic teaching.

He told a story about a shepherd who had a sheep run away. Anyone in the crowd who had ever worked with livestock understood the concepts he was talking about.

He told a story about woman who misplaced a precious coin, and anyone who had ever lost anything could relate.

He told a story about a man with two sons. One of the sons betrayed his father by taking his inheritance early and wasting it away. The other son was angry that his brother would have the audacity to come back and his father the audacity to welcome him back. Immediately anyone who heard the story who had ever betrayed or been betrayed listened up.

As we have studied the God Story we have seen that the Bible is not just a disconnected collection of historical accounts but a story. It is a story that connects us with the mysterious truths of God. Though it can be helpful at times to take a verse here or there, God wants us to connect with the whole story of the Bible.

Why do you think Jesus told stories instead of giving a lecture?

How can you share your story as a way of sharing the God Story with others?

*God, thank you for being present with me at all times. You have been with me in every life-changing moment, and I know you are here with me today. Help me to look for you in my story. Help me to hear how you are calling me into your story. In Jesus' name. Amen.*

# Day 2

The Inciting Incident is the moment in a story that kicks the whole thing into motion. It is where a story really gets going. It is that moment in the story when the main character's world is turned upside down and she begins the adventure of resolving all that has been shaken up. Everything has changed. The Inciting Incident is similar to a doorway through which the protagonist cannot return.[1] And you have to read on to see what happens.

For Abraham it was when his ninety-year-old wife became pregnant. For Joseph it was finding himself in the bottom of a hole. For Moses it was stumbling upon a bush that wouldn't burn up.

It can be tempting in these life-changing moments to immediately begin to think about how you can resolve all the issues that have arisen. The key to an Inciting Incident in the God Story is looking for where God is in the change and how God wants you to proceed.

Abraham saw his wife's pregnancy as the fulfillment of God's promise to him. Joseph saw the misfortune he faced as a way to honor God. Moses believed God could use him to be a part of the solution for his people.

If you look at the story of your life, what Inciting Incidents come to mind?

Where have you seen God in the changes in your life?

How is God calling you to live after some of these life-changing moments?

*God, thank you for being present with me at all times. You have been with me in every life-changing moment, and I know you are here with me today. Help me to look for you in my story. Help me to hear how you are calling me into your story. In Jesus' name. Amen.*

---

1. James Scott Bell elaborates on this concept of "doorways of no return" throughout his book *Plot & Structure* (Cincinnati: Writer's Digest Books, 2004).

# Day 3

The wandering people of God from the Exodus story did eventually make it to the land God had promised. Up to this point they had not been bound by any geographical barriers or physical boundaries. They were not connected because of a human leader. They were held together by their story and their God.

God was the common bond. God had been faithful to the promises of the journey. God had provided all they needed. And then, the people did something surprising. They asked for a king.

> One day the nation's leaders came to Samuel at Ramah and said, "You are an old man. You set a good example for your sons, but they haven't followed it. Now we want a king to be our leader, just like all the other nations. Choose one for us!"
> I Samuel 8:4-5 (CEV)

The people who never had a king because of their devotion to their God asked for a human ruler. Wasn't God enough?

Samuel tried to tell them the pitfalls of having a human king as their leader. But, at this point nothing could stop them; they had made up their minds.

Part of the God Story is the continuing thread of our desire to take things into our own hands and do it ourselves. Part of the God Story is the realization on our part that we can't go it alone. Part of the God Story is seeing that God is ready to take us back.

Who are you depending on today?

If you were to look at your life would it appear that you are relying more on yourself or God?

An early confession of the church was to claim Jesus as Lord. In a time when Caesar was the king, or "lord," the first Christians made a life-threatening claim that their king was Jesus. Today we often throw the phrase "Jesus is Lord" around with little thought of what it would truly mean for him to be king of our lives.

How do you see Jesus as the King of your life? Are there any areas of your life where you need to ask Jesus to be Lord?

*God, thank you for being present with me at all times. You have been with me in every life-changing moment, and I know you are here with me today. Help me to look for you in my story. Help me to hear how you are calling me into your story. In Jesus' name. Amen.*

# Day 4

Israel's great king experiment was a disaster. Their first king, Saul, started strong but eventually became insecure, paranoid, and self-focused.

So God sends Samuel to the home of Jesse to anoint a new king. Jesse has eight sons, one of them will be the heir to the throne. When Samuel arrives he sees the sons. They are tall, strong, and impressive. But, as each son stands before Samuel, God says "not that one…not that one…not that one."

Samuel asks, "are these all the sons you have" (1 Samuel 16:11)? Jesse remembers that his youngest son is out in the fields tending sheep. Samuel says, "Get him."

Out in the fields young David is spending a lazy day with the sheep. That is until he is summoned to stand before great Samuel in front of his father and older brothers.

God speaks, "He is the one."

David, the youngest of eight sons, stands before the old priest, the most revered man in the nation, who then takes a horn of oil and pours it over his dirty hair and face. The little shepherd boy who slept the night in the field will be the new king of Israel. The current king, though, is still alive and healthy. David is not his son, but God says this unlikely one will be the next ruler of God's people. Good story, huh?

This is David's Inciting Incident. Everything changes from this moment on. He steps through this doorway and he can't go back. We see Thread #4 in David's Inciting Incident:

*God calls the unlikely and gives them a better story.*

Throughout the God Story it is the unlikely that are chosen for the great God appointments. God uses the poor, the outcast, the rascal, the prostitute, and the rejected.

And if God uses them…God will use us. If God saw something in David, God sees something in you.

The God Story shows us that if you consider yourself one who is unlikely to be by God, then you will probably be used by God.

Why would you be an unlikely choice for God? How does it feel to know that God can use you despite the insufficiencies and inadequacies that you see?

*God, thank you for being present with me at all times. You have been with me in every life-changing moment, and I know you are here with me today. Help me to look for you in my story. Help me to hear how you are calling me into your story. In Jesus' name. Amen.*

# Day 5

Perhaps the most famous story of David is one that happens shortly after his anointing as the new king. Understand that David does not become the next king immediately after Samuel says it will be so. David waits years and years before the promise is fulfilled. After David is anointed as king he is sent back to the fields to tend sheep…again.

One day, though, David's father calls David in and sends him out to the battlefield where his older brothers are waging war against the Philistines. He sends David with food and hopes David will return with a message of assurance that his brothers are safe and sound.

Meanwhile, things are growing increasingly tense in the standoff between the Philistines and the Israelites. A Philistine champion, Goliath, a man over nine feet tall, each day challenges a warrior from the Israelite ranks to come out and fight him. Goliath says, "Whoever wins the fight wins the battle."

No Israelite even considered taking Goliath up on his contest.

Until David gets there.

David, a young boy, takes five stones and his sling and walks out to Goliath.

Goliath is not amused. He is insulted; he scoffs at this little challenger.

David acknowledges that he stands before him in the name of the Lord and it will be God who gives him victory.

David, puts a stone in his sling and throws it at the giant.

It hits him in the forehead, and Goliath the great falls to the ground. Dead.

David learns early in his story that nothing is too big for God. David learns that the best things you can be involved in are not battles that you can win on your own, but the one's where you have no hope unless God intervenes. David learned that the most rewarding things in life are the moments when you say, "God did it."

Where do you need God's miraculous power?

Imagine yourself on the other side of whatever battles you are facing saying, "God did it," and celebrating victory with God. Ask God to come intervene and do what only God can do.

*God, thank you for being present with me at all times. You have been with me in every life-changing moment, and I know you are here with me today. Help me to look for you in my story. Help me to hear how you are calling me into your story. In Jesus' name. Amen.*

# Day 6

When David was anointed as king it was a moment he would never forget. It was an Inciting Incident, a day when everything changed in his life.

David's life, though, would not be one glorious moment after another. He would encounter other Inciting Incidents that would leave him full of pain and regret. In other words, David made some serious mistakes.

In one part of his story, David becomes an adulterer, a murderer, and a liar. His sin is exposed and his life is changed forever. David's son then dies, and David would have had every reason to just throw in the towel. Sure, years before God had promised greatness for David, but that was before he squandered it all away.

But instead of growing bitter or hardened, David has a different reaction to his newfound situation.

He is broken. Utterly and totally broken. Instead of running away from God he runs to God.

He pleads with God:

> Please don't throw me out of your presence;
> please don't take your holy spirit away from me.
> Psalm 51:11

He begs God:

> Return the joy of your salvation to me and
>     sustain me with a willing spirit.

Psalm 51:12

He renews his promise to serve God:

> Then I will teach wrongdoers your ways,
>     and sinners will come back to you.

Psalm 51:13

David shows us that even when we have broken our promises to God, God is steadfast in God's promises to us. We turn to God and God has already turned to us.

God has a better story for us.

Psalm 51 is David's prayer of confession to God after his sin has been brought out into the open. Confession is a way of stepping back into God's better story for you. What do you need to confess to God today?

*God, thank you for being present with me at all times. You have been with me in every life-changing moment, and I know you are here with me today. Help me to look for you in my story. Help me to hear how you are calling me into your story. In Jesus' name. Amen.*

# Day 7

God calls the unlikely and gives them a better story.

Remember that the threads run throughout the whole God Story, so it should be no surprise that we see Jesus over and over again reaching out to the unlikely and giving them a better story.

> A man with leprosy came to [Jesus] and begged him on his knees, "If you are willing, you can make me clean." Jesus was indignant. He reached out his hand and touched the man. "I am willing," he said. "Be clean!" Immediately the leprosy left him and he was cleansed.
>
> Mark 1:40-42 (NIV)

Although verse 41 reads "Jesus was indignant" in this translation, it's important to note that many manuscripts translate that phrase as "Jesus was filled with compassion." The man with leprosy had lived his life as an outcast, pushed out of society, unwelcome to commune in the normal ways. Jesus spoke to him, touched him, and healed him. From that day forward the man would never be the same. He would no longer be the man with leprosy! He would need a new way to describe his life, a new story.

Jesus did this with a blind man, a woman who had a bleeding problem, tax collectors, common fishermen, the demon possessed, a prostitute, and on and on it goes. To each of them he gave a new story.

We have already considered how God calls us, the unlikely, and invites us into a better story. Today we must consider who the unlikely one is that we encounter who needs a better story.

Most likely we will intersect with someone today who needs a new story.

Ask God to give you eyes to see the one today whom you might share Christ's love with.

Consider how your story might be used to share the God Story with someone else.

You can help others walk through the doorway to connect with Jesus. It is a doorway they will never want to walk back through.

*God, thank you for being present with me at all times. You have been with me in every life-changing moment, and I know you are here with me today. Help me to look for you in my story. Help me to hear how you are calling me into your story. In Jesus' name. Amen.*

# Week 5: Soundtrack

*O God, open my ears to hear your voice. Open my heart to hear your song of joy being sung over me. Open my mouth to sing your praise. I give my life to you today. In Jesus' name. Amen.*

## Zephaniah 3:14-17

Rejoice, Daughter Zion! Shout, Israel!
  Rejoice and exult with all your heart, Daughter Jerusalem.
The Lord has removed your judgment;
  he has turned away your enemy.
The Lord, the king of Israel, is in your midst;
  you will no longer fear evil.
On that day, it will be said to Jerusalem:
  Don't fear, Zion.
  Don't let your hands fall.
The Lord your God is in your midst—a warrior bringing victory.
  He will create calm with his love;
  he will rejoice over you with singing.

# Day 1

It is something that you don't usually think about when you are watching a movie. Without it, though, something would be noticeably missing.

The Soundtrack, some would say, is as important as what you see. Not often noticed, it keeps the story moving and connects the beginning to the end.

Teenagers from the 1970s would only need a couple of notes to identify the theme song to *Jaws*. In the 1980s no one would mistake John Williams' score to *Star Wars*. In the 1990s, moviegoers can't imagine *Titanic* without Celine Dion's theme. More recently the Soundtrack to *Twilight* is one of the best-selling Soundtracks of all time.

No doubt you can hum even now the Soundtrack to your favorite movies.

We have been thinking about our lives as a story. Our lives are not just a disconnected set of events, but a part of a bigger epic novel—a feature film with adventure, intrigue, and suspense.

If so, what would be the Soundtrack to your story?

Who would sing? What instruments would need to be played?

Which leads me to another question: does the God Story have a Soundtrack?

What sounds do we hear? What melody connects Genesis to Revelation?

Zephaniah says that God will rejoice over us with singing.

What do you think that would sound like? What do you imagine God is singing over you?

It is hard to imagine that God might actually sing over us the way a parent would sing over a child. Yet, the God Story is not without a Soundtrack.

This week you will be encouraged to listen for the way the author of your story is delighting in you and even singing over you!

Keep your ears open today.

*O God, open my ears to hear your voice. Open my heart to hear your song of joy being sung over me. Open my mouth to sing your praise. I give my life to you today. In Jesus' name. Amen.*

# Day 2

Remember how the people of God asked God for a king? They were told it wasn't necessary, because God was their king and they didn't need a human one. Yet, they begged and begged, and God granted them their king.

It didn't go so well. The kingdom was split in two, and then there were two kings. Of most kings it would be said, "he did what was evil in the sight of the LORD" (2 Kings 21:2 NRSV). The great man-as-king experiment went very badly. Then other kings from other nations with more power and bigger armies came in and took over. The people of God were again subjugated to a foreign ruler who did know or worship their God. They were right back where they started: in need of forgiveness, in need of deliverance.

It was during this time that God raised up prophets. In the Old Testament sixteen books contain the story and words of these prophets. The word *prophet* derives from a Greek word that means to foresee. That is what we usually think about when we use the term *prophet*: one who sees the future. But to relegate prophets to fortunetelling only is to miss their true purpose.

The prophets' true task was to speak on behalf of God to the people, and to speak on behalf of the people to God.

Thread #1 said this: *God speaks because God desires rela-tionship.* The prophets would be God's mouthpiece in this time, God's voice singing over them.

The prophet says God still remembers God's promises. He sings that God desires for you to return. She gives voice to God's desire to welcome the people of God back.

Can you hear God singing that to you today?

*I'm here.*

*Return.*

*Come back to me.*

Listen to these words of God from the prophet Zechariah, "Return to me and I will return to you."

Over and over again God sings this over God's people, *Return to me and I will return to you.*

What does returning to God look like for you today?

*O God, open my ears to hear your voice. Open my heart to hear your song of joy being sung over me. Open my mouth to sing your praise. I give my life to you today. In Jesus' name. Amen.*

# Day 3

The prophets' voices provide a major piece of the sound-track to the God Story. Over the centuries God would raise up prophet after prophet who would speak of the promises of God to keep the people of God connected to the story.

You see, the people of God had in many ways forgotten the story. They worshipped other gods. They served other masters. They had many other idols. Life was hard and they went on with their lives and left the story of God and the God of their story behind.

We have the option to do life with no mind to the greater story too. It is easy to do. There is enough to consume us. There are bills to pay, appointments to make, and people to take care of.

The prophets in biblical times were an audible reminder that God is not content being left out! The prophets were the word of God for the people of God. They were a way for the people to hear God singing God's song of love and forgiveness and life.

Today one of the ways we hear God's voice is through God's word; we hear God through the story, through the Scriptures.

The Psalmist says God's word "is a light for my path" (Psalm 119:105).

God told Joshua not to let God's law "depart from your mouth, meditate on it day and night." (Joshua 1:8).

We need that daily reminder of God's presence in our lives and we hear that through God's word.

Jesus said that we can't live on bread alone but "on every word that comes from the mouth of God" (Matthew 4:4).

We can't make it on our own. We can't make it on what the world provides. We need to hear from God like we hear a Soundtrack throughout a movie. We hear it from beginning to end and it keeps us connected.

Do you have a regular commitment to hearing from God through the Scriptures?

If so, what does that look like? If not, what commitments would you like to make?

*O God, open my ears to hear your voice. Open my heart to hear your song of joy being sung over me. Open my mouth to sing your praise. I give my life to you today. In Jesus' name. Amen.*

# Day 4

Zephaniah was one of these reminding prophets. He lived approximately six centuries before Christ and about one hundred years after the prophets Micah and Nahum.

Israel had been defeated, and Jerusalem and the Temple had been destroyed. The nation of Judah was under fire from surrounding empires, and before long it too would be completely taken over.

The people desperately needed to hear from God.

Zephaniah says:

> The LORD your God is with you, he is mighty to save. He will take great delight in you; he will quiet you with his love, he will rejoice over you with singing.
>
> Zephaniah 3:17 (NIV)

Each part would be critical to hear for them. Each part is critical for us to hear today.

*God is with you.* The reminder that no matter what we are going through, God is present. We don't always have the answers to the "whys" and the "hows," but one thing we can be certain of; God is with us.

*He is mighty to save.* When we feel powerless, God has the power. When we look at the impossible situation, God sees possibilities. God is mighty and has the power to save us.

*He will take great delight in you.* This is where it gets interesting. God delights in us? This does not sound like a far-off God, but one who knows us intimately. Not only does God know and love us, but God delights in us. God's heart finds joy in you and in me.

*He will quiet you with his love.* Love can do a lot of things. Here Zephaniah says God's love can calm us down, quiet our hearts. Do you need that today?

*He will rejoice over you with singing.* The God of the universe, the God who created heaven and earth, sings over you with joy. The sight of you causes God to hum and then burst into song. I'm not making this stuff up. God's voice is the Soundtrack over your life singing of the promise of God's presence, God's power that can rescue you from any danger, and God's love that calms your heart and quiets your soul.

Which part of this song is hardest for you to hear?

Which is easiest?

*O God, open my ears to hear your voice. Open my heart to hear your song of joy being sung over me. Open my mouth to sing your praise. I give my life to you today. In Jesus' name. Amen.*

# Day 5

It's kind of hard to take in, this belief that God sings over us. Is this just somebody romanticizing and getting all touchy-feely about God?

Zephaniah is not a romantic book. This is not the Song of Solomon. Zephaniah's account is a hard one. It exposes the depth of betrayal of the people, how far they have turned from God, and the devastating consequences of these choices.

So, when you hear about God delighting, quieting, and singing over us, please understand the context. God is saying this to people who have run away from God, forgotten about God, left the God Story behind.

Zephaniah is introducing us to Thread #5 in the God Story: *God's love is recurring and relentless.*

Like a Soundtrack, God's love runs throughout the story. It is a love that is relentless in the pursuit of God's beloved.

Have you ever experienced re-occurring, relentless love from someone else? Write briefly how that love made you feel.

Is it hard for you to imagine that kind of love coming from God? Or do you accept God's unconditional love more easily?

Zephaniah did all that he could to get this message to the people because he knew that they needed to hear it. They needed to know there was a God that had not given up on them, and more than that God had a love for them that causes God to burst into song over them.

Take a moment to consider the kind of love that God has for you. Carry that love with you today.

*O God, open my ears to hear your voice. Open my heart to hear your song of joy being sung over me. Open my mouth to sing your praise. I give my life to you today. In Jesus' name. Amen.*

# Day 6

When I hear the Zephaniah verse about a God who sings over us, I am reminded of a night I was stuck on the interstate.

Rachel and I were new parents. We had an almost two-year-old little girl who had become everything to us. We had planned a day-long trip to a nearby city. On our return drive home, just a few miles outside of the city, traffic came to a complete standstill. There was an accident. We turned off our car and sat in the dark. Just minutes before, Mary had finally closed her eyes and fallen asleep. After a day in the city, she needed the sleep desperately, and we needed her to sleep desperately.

Suddenly, emergency vehicles sped by our window and woke her up. She went into an immediate meltdown. You know the two-year-old *I'm so tired, I'm out of my element,* meltdown. I wanted to have one too.

Rachel calmly got Mary out of her car seat, held her in her lap, and began to rock an shush her the way a mother does her baby.

Rachel said, "Listen Mary, don't you hear it?"

I didn't hear anything.

Rachel continued, "Don't you hear the crickets?"

I hadn't noticed it before, but now that we had our windows down you could indeed hear the sound of hundreds of crickets in the woods singing in the night.

Rachel said to Mary, "Don't you hear what they are singing? It's ok, it's ok, it's ok, it's ok."

Mary calmed down, I did too, and we sat together in the dark until the road was cleared. You know, with kids you have to repeat things over and over again.

It's ok, it's ok, it's ok, it's ok.

The voice of the prophets is God's Soundtrack; God saying over and over again, "It's ok."

I'm with you. I'm mighty to save. I delight in you.

I want to quiet you when you are near meltdown or out of your element.

God's love for us is sung in the opening credits and throughout the whole story until the end. Recurring and relentless.

*O God, open my ears to hear your voice. Open my heart to hear your song of joy being sung over me. Open my mouth to sing your praise. I give my life to you today. In Jesus' name. Amen.*

# Day 7

The last book in the Bible is Revelation. It is a mysterious book, and it describes some of the things that will happen at the end of the God Story here on earth.

It turns out, there will be a lot of singing.

I guess it shouldn't surprise us, since we have a God who has been singing over us for so long.

But, it looks like in the end we will be the ones singing.

There will be a great mass choir singing, "Hallelujah! Salvation and glory and power belong to our God" (Revelation 19:1 NIV).

When it all is said and done and there are no more tears and no more pain, why wouldn't we sing?

Why wouldn't our voices join together and sing of the greatness and mercy and love of our God who never gave up on us?

These songs of praise, though, don't have to wait to be sung. We are to sing them here as a way of reminding ourselves of our great God and pointing others to the one who desires them too.

What song of praise would you write to God today?

*O God, open my ears to hear your voice. Open my heart to hear your song of joy being sung over me. Open my mouth to sing your praise. I give my life to you today. In Jesus' name. Amen.*

# Week 6:
# Waiting for Resolution

*God, I am still waiting for Resolution in some areas of my life. Remind me that you wait with me. Remind me that you have good in store for me. Help me to trust in you as the author of the story and to wait faithfully. I wait expectantly to see the beautiful things you want to do in my story. In the name of Jesus our Savior. Amen.*

## John 12:12-19

The next day the great crowd that had come for the festival heard that Jesus was coming to Jerusalem. They took palm branches and went out to meet him. They shouted,

> "Hosanna!
> *Blessings on the one who comes in the name of the Lord!*
> Blessings on the king of Israel!"

Jesus found a young donkey and sat on it, just as it is written,
*Don't be afraid, Daughter Zion.*

> *Look! Your king is coming,*
> *sitting on a donkey's colt.*

His disciples didn't understand these things at first. After he was glorified, they remembered that these things had been written about him and that they had done these things to him.

The crowd who had been with him when he called Lazarus out of the tomb and raised him from the dead were testifying about him. That's why the crowd came to meet him, because they had heard about this miraculous sign that he had done. Therefore, the Pharisees said to each other, "See! You've accomplished nothing! Look! The whole world is following him!"

# Day 1

Y ou may remember from school the simple graph that
shows the structure of a story.

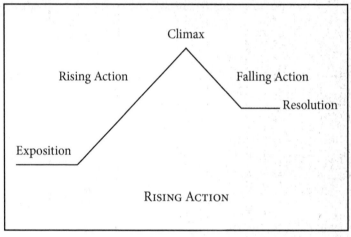

After a story reaches its climax, it moves towards Resolution.
Resolution is where everything is wrapped up neatly.
Everything falls into place, and we get the answers we were
waiting for.

Much of our life is found waiting for Resolution. We wait for
the deal to come through, for the illness to end, for the relationship to get better. We wait for Resolution.

Much of the God Story finds its characters waiting for Resolution. Abraham waits for the son that was promised to him. The Israelites wait to enter the Promised Land. The Israelites call out for a king, but it turns out the kings they get are not the kings they truly need. So, they begin to wait for *the* King, the Messiah, the one who will make all things right.

They wait for centuries. When will he come? When will we be set free? When will the pain end? They're waiting for Resolution.

Being faithful involves waiting. Waiting is hard!

What are you waiting for? Where do you need Resolution?

Have you ever thought about your waiting as an expression of your faith in God, that waiting faithfully is a way to honor God and point others to God?

How do you think you can honor God in your current waiting?

*God, I am still waiting for Resolution in some areas of my life. Remind me that you wait with me. Remind me that you have good in store for me. Help me to trust in you as the author of the story and to wait faithfully. I wait expectantly to see the beautiful things you want to do in my story. In the name of Jesus our Savior. Amen.*

# Day 2

You know that feeling you get after you have waited fifteen, then twenty minutes longer than you should have for either your table to be ready at a restaurant or your car to be finished at the auto shop?

When Jesus rode into Jerusalem on a little donkey on that Sunday afternoon, the people of God had been waiting for the Messiah for centuries.

They were more than a little ready for this to happen.

And there are plenty of moments in the God Story when the people get it wrong, but this is one of those moments when they get it right. They give Jesus a king's welcome. They laud and applaud him like you should the Messiah. They throw their coats on the ground, wave branches in the air and say, "Blessed is he who comes in the name of the Lord!" (John 12:13 NIV).

They also cry, "Hosanna!"

*Hosanna* is not a word used much in our common vernacular. *Hosanna* when it is used it in the church is often used as a statement of praise and adoration. It has certainly become that. The word, though, really means "Save us."

And even more literally it could have meant "Save now."

We can't wait any longer. We need you now. Wrap this up. Hosanna. Save us now.

There comes that point in any good story when you are longing for Resolution and you just can't wait anymore. If you could you would beg the author, the director, whoever is in charge to give us Resolution.

The people gathered on the streets in Jerusalem had waited long enough and even though they did not fully understand who Jesus was, something said that he might be the one, and they cried out for Resolution. Save us now.

*Save* is not a word we use much in our common vernacular unless we are referring to saving data on our computer. But, most of us are in need of being saved from something. We are all in need of a Savior.

What do you need saving from?

*God, I am still waiting for Resolution in some areas of my life. Remind me that you wait with me. Remind me that you have good in store for me. Help me to trust in you as the author of the story and to wait faithfully. I wait expectantly to see the beautiful things you want to do in my story. In the name of Jesus our Savior. Amen.*

# Day 3

It was a broken community of broken people who gathered on the streets of Jerusalem on Palm Sunday. They waved branches and cried out "Save us!"

It is the broken who need Resolution.

I will never forget when Ava died. Ava was the two-year-old daughter of an old friend of mine. When she died there was no good reason and no good answers. The night after her death, a hundred or more of us gathered in a church on a Monday night. We stood there holding hands and people voiced their prayers to God. They weren't eloquent but they were real. They came from a broken place to a God who we hoped could somehow save this situation.

It was one of the most real moments in my life. To stand there, clutching hands with a community that was broken because something terrible had happened. As those prayers concluded, the pastor invited me to come and end the prayer time. I felt inadequate for the task. I had come as a grieving friend that night, not as a pastor. And so I came to the microphone, and something that is rare for me happened: I could think of nothing to say. I looked out at the crowd, still holding hands, old people, young people, babies making baby noises. The only words that could come out of my mouth were "We need you."

"God, if ever we've needed you, we need you. We need you now."

I walked out, still waiting for Resolution.

Strangely, that's how I picture the palm waving parade that day. It appears at first glance to be a celebration, but listen again to what they were shouting. Save us. Save us now.

I hear, "We need you. God, if ever we've needed you, we need you now."

To all broken communities of people, He comes. To broken marriages, He comes. To broken finances, He comes. To broken churches, He comes. To broken nations, He comes. He comes, and by the end of the week we have forgotten and we cry out, "Crucify!" And you know what?

He comes again.

What situation do you desperately need Jesus to come into today?

*God, I am still waiting for Resolution in some areas of my life. Remind me that you wait with me. Remind me that you have good in store for me. Help me to trust in you as the author of the story and to wait faithfully. I wait expectantly to see the beautiful things you want to do in my story. In the name of Jesus our Savior. Amen.*

# Day 4

We have talked about the inevitability of uncertainty in our stories. In a story, you don't know what's coming next. You have to turn the page to find out.

A good storyteller lets you know that you are getting close to a monumental, story-changing moment. Like your first kiss, the first time to hold your grandchild, or that hike to the bottom of the Grand Canyon, there are some big days that you can see coming, and they are as good as advertised. A good storyteller lets you know leading up to the big day that you need to read slowly and pay attention because what is coming next will shape the character forever.

Everything about Jesus' life on earth was leading up to this week in Jerusalem. As we read the story we know that something big is going to happen there. After Jesus' welcome when he rides in to Jerusalem we think everything is happening the way we hoped. Jesus finally is getting his due. He is the King.

Then we feel the rug pulled out from under us as Sunday turns into Friday. The same crowd that shouted "Save us!" now cries "Crucify!" Jesus is betrayed by those who knew him best. Jesus is handed over to the authorities.

We want to stop reading, but we can't. Jesus is humiliated, beaten, and killed.

We learn that the big days don't always go the way we expected.

There are few of us who are immune from major disappointments in life. Most of us can think of times when our expectations were not met. Many of us have experienced great tragedy when we did not see it coming.

As we move toward the Resurrection story, let us pause today and think of the major disappointments. Can you relate to the disciples who saw a big day turn upside down and become their worst nightmare?

What disappointments still linger in your heart?

God includes tragedy in the story, so we can see our stories in the God Story. God acknowledges and embraces our disappointment, our loss as we see God's great loss in the death of Jesus.

*God, I am still waiting for Resolution in some areas of my life. Remind me that you wait with me. Remind me that you have good in store for me. Help me to trust in you as the author of the story and to wait faithfully. I wait expectantly to see the beautiful things you want to do in my story. In the name of Jesus our Savior. Amen.*

# Day 5

Early in the morning of the first day of the week, while it was still dark, Mary Magdalene came to the tomb and saw that the stone had been taken away from the tomb.

John 20:1

For Mary the story was over. She had found hope and life in Jesus, and now all of that was done. Jesus himself had said, "It is finished." Mary figured her life was finished too.

She came to the tomb because what else was there to do?

We wish there was something to be done with the ache, and the pain. We have to go somewhere. The grave site signifies that it is over; it is done. We use immovable stones to signify the finality of it all.

Mary sees that the stone has been moved. She assumes someone has stolen the body. So, she cries. She stays and cries. She cries and stays. The Jesus run is over. His life is done. Is her life done?

And then, suddenly she's not alone. You know the feeling when you think you're alone and then you realize you're not? It's unsettling. You put your guard up; you become very aware of your surroundings. Your brain tries to make sense of it quickly. Mary is in a garden so she assumes the man behind her is the gardener.

"If you have taken his body somewhere, it's ok, just let me know where he is, and I will get it. You're not in trouble; just tell me where he is!"

And then…"Mary," he says. And she knew. Just like you know it's your mom when she says your name on the phone. Just like you know it's your child when he calls to you from down the hall. She knew. It wasn't over. It wasn't done. He wasn't gone. He wasn't dead. It was Jesus.

It's called a Twist Ending. The story takes a turn that no one saw coming, but it is the only thing that could make sense of it all. All great stories have one. When all hope is lost, the unthinkable happens.

It's why you must hold out hope if you find yourself if in a situation where you see no way out. You are a part of the God Story, and your God has the power to do something you never expected to save you.

God did that in Jesus for you.

The God Story shows us that God is not done. Jesus is not dead. Because He lives, you live.

*God, I am still waiting for Resolution in some areas of my life. Remind me that you wait with me. Remind me that you have good in store for me. Help me to trust in you as the author of the story and to wait faithfully. I wait expectantly to see the beautiful things you want to do in my story. In the name of Jesus our Savior. Amen.*

# Day 6

R ead the resurrection account from John 20:1-18:

Early in the morning of the first day of the week, while it was still dark, Mary Magdalene came to the tomb and saw that the stone had been taken away from the tomb. She ran to Simon Peter and the other disciple, the one whom Jesus loved, and said, "They have taken the Lord from the tomb, and we don't know where they've put him." Peter and the other disciple left to go to the tomb. They were running together, but the other disciple ran faster than Peter and was the first to arrive at the tomb. Bending down to take a look, he saw the linen cloths lying there, but he didn't go in. Following him, Simon Peter entered the tomb and saw the linen cloths lying there. He also saw the face cloth that had been on Jesus' head. It wasn't with the other clothes but was folded up in its own place. Then the other disciple, the one who arrived at the tomb first, also went inside. He saw and believed. They didn't yet understand the scripture that Jesus must rise from the dead. Then the disciples returned to the place where they were staying.

Mary stood outside near the tomb, crying. As she cried, she bent down to look into the tomb. She saw two angels dressed in white, seated where the body of Jesus had been, one at the head and one at the foot. The angels asked her, "Woman, why are you crying?"

She replied, "They have taken away my Lord, and I don't know where they've put him." As soon as she had said this, she turned around and saw Jesus standing there, but she didn't know it was Jesus.

Jesus said to her, "Woman, why are you crying? Who are you looking for?"

Thinking he was the gardener, she replied, "Sir, if you have carried him away, tell me where you have put him and I will get him."

Jesus said to her, "Mary."

She turned and said to him in Aramaic, "Rabbouni" (which means Teacher).

Jesus said to her, "Don't hold on to me, for I haven't yet gone up to my Father. Go to my brothers and sisters and tell them, 'I'm going up to my Father and your Father, to my God and your God.'"

Mary Magdalene left and announced to the disciples, "I've seen the Lord." Then she told them what he said to her.

If you had been one of Jesus first followers, how would you have reacted to the empty tomb? What would you have done?

Mary, Peter, and John are entrusted with telling people of Jesus' resurrection. They had to tell the story. How can you tell the story of what God has done through Jesus Christ?

*God, I am still waiting for Resolution in some areas of my life. Remind me that you wait with me and that you have good in store for me. Help me wait faithfully and to trust you as the author of the story. I wait expectantly to see the beautiful things you want to do in my story. In the name of Jesus our Savior. Amen.*

# Day 7

R ead the resurrection account from Luke 24:1-12:

Very early in the morning on the first day of the week, the women went to the tomb, bringing the fragrant spices they had prepared. They found the stone rolled away from the tomb, but when they went in, they didn't find the body of the Lord Jesus. They didn't know what to make of this. Suddenly, two men were standing beside them in gleaming bright clothing. The women were frightened and bowed their faces toward the ground, but the men said to them, "Why do you look for the living among the dead? He isn't here, but has been raised. Remember what he told you while he was still in Galilee, that the Human One must be handed over to sinners, be crucified, and on the third day rise again." Then they remembered his words. When they returned from the tomb, they reported all these things to the eleven and all the others. It was Mary Magdalene, Joanna, Mary the mother of James, and the other women with them who told these things to the apostles. Their words struck the apostles as nonsense, and they didn't believe the women. But Peter ran to the tomb. When he bent over to look inside, he saw only the linen cloth. Then he returned home, wondering what had happened.

Looking back at yesterday's reading from John what strikes you about the differences in the two accounts?

With all the amazing things that disciples had seen Jesus do, why do you think they had trouble believing in Jesus' resurrection?

What do you have trouble believing about God?

From the beginning, the God Story has been heading toward the resurrection of Jesus. The God Story does not, though, end there. Your life is the continuation of the story of the people of God.

How will you live differently knowing that you are a character in the greatest story ever?

*God, I am still waiting for Resolution in some areas of my life. Remind me that you wait with me. Remind me that you have good in store for me. Help me to trust in you as the author of the story and to wait faithfully. I wait expectantly to see the beautiful things you want to do in my story. In the name of Jesus our Savior. Amen.*